A Jane Austen Miscellany

A Jane Austen Miscellany

Sisters ❧ Suitors ❧ Families ❧ Friends

EDITED BY
KRISTEN MARÉE CLEARY AND
ROBIN LANGLEY SOMMER

DOVETAIL
BOOKS

ISBN 0-9636673-8-6

Printed in China

9 8 7 6 5 4 3 2 1

for

MAMA AND PAPA

CONTENTS

$\mathcal{F}$OREWORD

$\mathcal{E}$ntertaining as they are, Jane Austen's novels also convey eloquently the virtues of love, honesty and thoughtfulness, as they condemn the sins of hypocrisy and deceit and the social context that breeds them. This anthology of a peerless writer's observations on the human experience highlights her characteristic sharpness and wit, and also shows the gentleness and integrity expressed through many of her characters. Heroes, heroines, rakes and debutantes, maiden aunts and family retainers all play their part in the rich and vivid tapestry of social comedy woven by Jane Austen almost 200 years ago and still delighting us today. ❦ ❦ ❦

Sisters

The strength of the relationships between some of the sisters in Jane Austen's works mirrors the close relationship Austen enjoyed with her own sister. These bonds are based on mutual affection and respect, and they withstand any adversity.

ℛEFLECTED HAPPINESS

As Elizabeth had no longer any interest of her own to pursue, she turned her attention almost entirely on her sister and Mr. Bingley, and the train of agreeable reflections which her observations gave birth to made her perhaps almost as happy as Jane. She saw her in idea settled in that very house in all the felicity which a marriage of true affection can bestow; and she felt capable under such circumstances even to like Mr. Bingley's two sisters.

ELIZABETH ON JANE BENNET
Pride and Prejudice

$\mathcal{A}$ COMPLEMENTARY TRIO

Elinor, this eldest daughter whose advice was so effectual, possessed a strength of understanding, and coolness of judgment, which qualified her, though only nineteen, to be the counsellor of her mother....She had an excellent heart;—her disposition was affectionate, and her feelings were strong; but she knew how to govern them: it was a knowledge which her mother had yet to learn and which one of her sisters had resolved never to be taught.

Marianne's abilities were, in many respects, quite equal to Elinor's. She was sensible and clever; but eager in every thing; her sorrows, her joys, could have no moderation. She was generous, amiable, interesting: she was every thing but prudent. The resemblance between her and her mother was strikingly great.

Margaret, the other sister, was a good humoured well disposed girl; but as she had already imbibed a good deal of Marianne's romance, without having much of her sense, she did not, at thirteen, bid fair to equal her sisters at a more advanced period of life.

ON THE DASHWOOD SISTERS
Sense and Sensibility

AFFECTIONATE TEASING

"It has been a very agreeable day," said Miss Bennet [Jane] to Elizabeth. "The party seemed so well selected, so suitable one with the other. I hope we may often meet again."

Elizabeth smiled.

"Lizzy, you must not do so. You must not suspect me. It mortifies me. I assure you that I have now learned to enjoy his conversation as an agreeable and sensible young man, without having a wish beyond it. I am perfectly satisfied from what his manners now are that he never had any design of engaging my affection. It is only that he is blessed with greater sweetness of address, and a stronger desire of generally pleasing, than any other man."

"You are very cruel," said her sister, "you will not let me smile, and are provoking me to it every moment."

"How hard it is in some cases to be believed!"

"And how impossible in others!"

"But why should you wish to persuade me that I feel more than I acknowledge?"

"That is a question which I hardly know how to answer. We all love to instruct, though we teach only what is not worth knowing. Forgive me; and if you persist in indifference, do not make *me* your confidant."

ELIZABETH AND JANE BENNET ON MR. BINGLEY
Pride and Prejudice

SISTERLY CONCERN

Elinor, in spite of every occasional doubt of Willoughby's constancy, could not witness the rapture of delightful expectation which filled the whole soul and beamed in the eyes of Marianne, without feeling how blank was her own prospect, how cheerless her own state of mind in the comparison, and how gladly she would engage in the solicitude of Marianne's situation to have the same animating object in view, the same possibility of hope. A short, a very short time, however, must now decide what Willoughby's intentions were; in all probability, he was already in town. Marianne's eagerness to be gone declared her dependence on finding him there; and Elinor was resolved not only upon gaining every new light as to his character which her own observation or the intelligence of others could give her, but likewise upon watching his behaviour to her sister with such zealous attention, as to ascertain what he was and what he meant, before any meetings had taken place. Should the result of her observations be unfavourable, she was determined at all events to open the eyes of her sister; should it be otherwise, her exertions would be of a very different nature — she must then learn to avoid every selfish comparison, and banish every regret which might lessen her satisfaction in the happiness of Marianne.

ON ELINOR AND MARIANNE DASHWOOD
Sense and Sensibility

Admiration and approbation

"My dear Jane!" exclaimed Elizabeth, "you are too good. Your sweetness and disinterestedness are really angelic; I do not know what to say to you. I feel as if I have never done you justice, or loved you as you deserve."

Miss Bennet eagerly disclaimed all extraordinary merit, and threw back the praise on her sister's warm affection.

"Nay," said Elizabeth, "this is not fair. *You* wish to think all the world respectable and are hurt if I speak ill of anybody. *I* only want to think *you* perfect, and you set yourself against it. Do not be afraid of my running into any excess, of my encroaching on your privilege of universal goodwill. You need not. There are few people whom I really love, and still fewer of whom I think well."

> ELIZABETH AND JANE BENNET
> ON JANE'S CHARACTER
> *Pride and Prejudice*

SHARING A MOMENT OF JOY

Jane could have no reserves from Elizabeth, where confidence would give pleasure; and instantly embracing her, acknowledged, with the liveliest emotion, that she was the happiest creature in the world.

"'Tis too much!" she added, "by far too much. I do not deserve it. Oh! why is not everybody as happy?"

Elizabeth's congratulations were given with a sincerity, a warmth, a delight, which words could but poorly express. Every sentence of kindness was a fresh source of happiness to Jane.…

"I am certainly the most fortunate creature that ever existed!" cried Jane. "Oh! Lizzy, why am I thus singled from my family, and blessed above them all. If I could but see *you* as happy! If there *were* but such another man for you!"

"If you were to give me forty such men, I could never be so happy as you. Till I have your disposition, your goodness, I never can have your happiness."

> ELIZABETH AND JANE BENNET
> UPON JANE'S ENGAGEMENT
> *Pride and Prejudice*

*A*DOLESCENT FRIENDS AND COMPANIONS

Catherine's heart was affectionate, her disposition cheerful and open, without conceit or affectation of any kind; her manners just removed from the awkwardness and shyness of a girl; her person pleasing, and when in good looks, pretty; and her mind about as ignorant and uninformed as the female mind at seventeen usually is. Sally, or rather Sarah (for what young lady of common gentility will reach the age of sixteen without altering her name as far as she can?), must from situation be at this time the intimate friend and confidante of her sister [then departing for a visit to Bath]. It is remarkable, however, that she neither insisted on Catherine's writing by every post, nor exacted her promise of transmitting the character of every new acquaintance, nor a detail of every interesting conversation that Bath might produce.

CATHERINE AND SALLY MORLAND
Northanger Abbey

SISTERHOOD AFTER MARRIAGE

Between [the households at] Barton and Delaford, there was that constant communication which strong family affection would naturally dictate; and among the merits and the happiness of Elinor and Marianne, let it not be ranked as the least considerable, that though sisters, and living almost within sight of each other, they could live without disagreement between themselves, or producing coolness between their husbands.

ON ELINOR AND MARIANNE DASHWOOD
Sense and Sensibility

Not everyone enjoys the good fortune of having supportive, open and affectionate siblings. Often, relationships between sisters are strained by petty rivalries, selfishness or simple incompatibility.

$\mathcal{A}$N ILL-ASSORTED SISTERHOOD

Though better endowed than the elder sister [Elizabeth, vain and superficial], Mary had not Anne's understanding nor temper. While well, and happy, and properly attended to, she had great good humour and excellent spirits; but any indisposition sunk her completely. She had no resources for solitude; and, inheriting a considerable share of the Elliot self-importance, was very prone to add to every other distress that of fancying herself neglected and ill-used. In person, she was inferior to both sisters, and had, even in her bloom, only reached the dignity of being 'a fine girl'.

THE THREE ELLIOT SISTERS
Persuasion

ℰSTRANGEMENT

To save herself from useless remonstrance, Mrs. Price [Fanny Ward] never wrote to her family on the subject till actually married [against their advice]. Lady Bertram [Maria Ward], who was a woman of very tranquil feelings, and a temper remarkably easy and indolent, would have contented herself with merely giving up her sister, and thinking no more of the matter; but Mrs. Norris [the eldest sister] had a spirit of activity, which could not be satisfied till she had written a long and angry letter to Fanny, to point out the folly of her conduct, and threaten her with all its possible ill consequences. Mrs. Price, in her turn, was injured and angry; and an answer, which comprehended each sister in its bitterness, and bestowed such very disrespectful reflections on the pride of Sir Thomas [Bertram], as Mrs. Norris could not possibly keep to herself, put an end to all intercourse between them for a considerable period.

THE WARD SISTERS, DIVIDED BY MARRIAGE
Mansfield Park

C OLD CALCULATIONS

Of all the family, Mary was probably the one most immediately gratified by the circumstance [of Anne's engagement to Captain Wentworth]. It was creditable to have a sister married, and she might flatter herself with having been greatly instrumental to the connection, by keeping Anne with her in the autumn; and as her own sister must be better than her husband's sisters, it was very agreeable that Captain Wentworth should be a richer man than either Captain Benwick or Charles Hayter. She had something to suffer, perhaps, when they came into contact again, in seeing Anne restored to the rights of seniority, and the mistress of a very pretty laundaulette; but she had a future to look forward to of powerful consolation. Anne had no Uppercross Hall before her, no landed estate, no headship of a family; and if they could but keep Captain Wentworth from being made a baronet, she would not change situations with Anne.

It would be well for the eldest sister [Elizabeth] if she were equally satisfied with her situation, for a change is not very probable there. She had soon the mortification of seeing [her cousin] Mr. Elliot withdraw, and no one of proper condition has since presented himself to raise even the unfounded hopes which sunk with him.

THE ELLIOT SISTERS, UPON ANNE'S ENGAGEMENT
Persuasion

Perfect foils

Very, very happy were both Elizabeth and Anne Elliot as they walked in. Elizabeth, arm-in-arm with Miss Carteret, and looking on the broad back of the Dowager Viscountess Dalrymple before, had nothing to wish for which did not seem within her reach; and Anne—but it would be an insult to the nature of Anne's felicity to draw any comparison between it and her sister's; the origin of one all selfish vanity, of the other all generous attachment.

ELIZABETH AND ANNE ELLIOT
Persuasion

CHARACTER FORMATION AND ITS OPPOSITE

It was not very wonderful that, with all their promising talents and early information, [Maria and Julia Bertram] should be entirely deficient in the less common acquirements of self-knowledge, generosity and humility. In everything but disposition, they were admirably taught. Sir Thomas did not know what was wanting, because, though a truly anxious father, he was not outwardly affectionate, and the reserve of his manner repressed all the flow of their spirits before him.

To the education of her daughters Lady Bertram paid not the smallest attention. She had not time for such cares. She was a woman who spent her days in sitting, nicely dressed, on a sofa, doing some long piece of needlework, of little use and no beauty, thinking more of her pug than her children, but very indulgent to the latter, when it did not put herself to inconvenience.

ON MARIA AND JULIA BERTRAM
Mansfield Park

· II ·

Suitors

A Jane Austen Miscellany

In Jane Austen's world, an unmarried woman—and her family—often assess a suitor primarily in terms of his social and financial status. In the novels, such scenarios are sometimes reminiscent of a marketplace, where the best goods go to the most determined buyer. Emotional responses can play a negligible role in courtship.

A PREDICTABLE MATCH

Now it so happened, that, in spite of Emma's resolution of never marrying, there was something in the name, in the idea, of Mr. Frank Churchill, which always interested her. She had frequently thought—especially since his father's marriage with Miss Taylor—that if she were to marry, he was the very person to suit her in age, character and condition. He seemed, by this connection between the families, quite to belong to her. She could not but suppose it to be a match that everybody who knew them must think of.

EMMA WOODHOUSE REFLECTS ON HER FUTURE
Emma

$\mathcal{E}$LIGIBLE QUALITIES

Mr. Bingley was good-looking and gentlemanlike; he had a pleasant countenance, and easy unaffected manners. His sisters were fine women, with an air of decided fashion. His brother-in-law, Mr. Hurst, merely looked the gentleman; but his friend Mr. Darcy soon drew the attention of the room by his fine, tall person, handsome features, noble mien—and the report which was in general circulation within five minutes after his entrance of his having ten thousand a year. The gentlemen pronounced him to be a fine figure of a man, the ladies declared he was much handsomer than Mr. Bingley, and he was looked at with great admiration for about half the evening.

> AT THE MERYTON ASSEMBLY
> *Pride and Prejudice*

IN THE MARKET

It is a truth universally acknowledged that a single man in possession of a good fortune must be in want of a wife.

> OPENING SENTENCE
> *Pride and Prejudice*

*A*N EARLY ATTACHMENT

[Captain Wentworth] was, at that time, a remarkably fine young man, with a great deal of intelligence, spirit, and brilliancy; and Anne an extremely pretty girl, with gentleness, modesty, taste, and feeling. Half the sum of attraction, on either side, might have been enough, for he had nothing to do, and she had hardly anybody to love; but the encounter of such lavish recommendations could not fail.

> ON CAPTAIN WENTWORTH'S AND
> ANNE ELLIOT'S FIRST ENGAGEMENT
> *Persuasion*

*F*IRST IMPRESSIONS OF A STRANGER

They made their appearance in the Lower Rooms; and here fortune was more favourable to our heroine [Catherine Morland]. The master of the ceremonies introduced her to a very gentleman-like young man as a partner; his name was Tilney. He seemed to be about four or five and twenty, was rather tall, had a pleasing countenance, a very intelligent and lively eye, and, if not quite handsome, was very near it….

His name was not in the Pump Room book, and curiosity could do no more. He must be gone from Bath; yet he had not mentioned that his stay would be so short. This sort of mysteriousness, which is always so becoming in a hero, threw a fresh grace, in Catherine's imagination, around his person and manners, and increased her anxiety to know more of him.

> ON HENRY TILNEY
> *Northanger Abbey*

The strong women who comprise Austen's central characters provide sharp commentary on the cynical calculations of the marriage market. Before finding true love, these heroines often suffer the attentions of the most undesirable, and persistent, suitors.

*P*RE-EMPTING THE ANSWER

"My reasons for marrying are, first, that I think it a right thing for every clergyman in easy circumstances (like myself) to set the example of matrimony in his parish. Secondly, that I am convinced it will add very greatly to my happiness; and thirdly, which perhaps I ought to have mentioned earlier, that it is the particular advice and recommendation of the very noble lady whom I have the honour of calling patroness. Twice has she condescended to give me her opinion (unasked too!) on this subject.…Allow me, by the way, to observe, my fair cousin, that I do not reckon the notice and kindness of Lady Catherine de Bourgh as among the least of the advantages in my power to offer."

[Elizabeth determinedly refuses Mr. Collins.]

"You must give me leave to flatter myself, my dear cousin, that your refusal of my addresses is merely words of course. My reasons for believing it are briefly these: it does not appear to me that my hand is unworthy of your acceptance, or that the establishment I can offer would be any other than highly desirable. My situation in life, my connections with the family of de Bourgh, and my relationship to your own, are circumstances highly in my favor; and you should take it into further consideration that in spite of your manifold attractions, it is by no means certain that another offer of marriage may ever be made to you. Your portion is unhappily so small that it will in all likelihood undo the effects of your loveliness and amiable qualifications. As I must therefore conclude that you are not serious in your rejection of me, I shall choose to attribute it to your wish of increasing my love by suspense, according to the usual practice of elegant females."

MR. COLLINS'S PROPOSAL TO ELIZABETH BENNET
Pride and Prejudice

Unwelcome Attentions

Jealousy of Mr. Elliot! It was the only intelligible motive. Captain Wentworth jealous of her affection! Could she have believed it a week ago; three hours ago! For a moment the gratification was exquisite. But, alas! there were very different thoughts to succeed. How was such jealousy to be quieted? How was the truth to reach him? How, in all the peculiar disadvantages of their respective situations, would he ever learn her real sentiments? It was misery to think of Mr. Elliot's attentions. Their evil was incalculable.

> ANNE ELLIOT'S SUITORS
> *Persuasion*

Mutual Disregard

Maria, with only Mr. Rushworth to attend her, [was] doomed to the repeated details of his day's sport, good or bad, his boast of his dogs, his jealousy of his neighbours, his doubts of their [hunting] qualifications, and his zeal after poachers—subjects which will not find their way into female feelings without some talent on one side, or some attachment on the other.

> ON MARIA BERTRAM AND MR. RUSHWORTH
> *Mansfield Park*

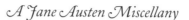
*A*N OVERBEARING ADVANCE

Scarcely had they passed the sweep-gate and joined the other carriage, than she found her subject cut up—her hand seized—her attention demanded, and Mr. Elton actually making violent love to her: availing himself of the precious opportunity, declaring sentiments which must already be known, hoping—fearing—adoring—ready to die if she refused him; but flattering himself that his ardent attachment and unequalled love and unexampled passion could not fail of having some effect, and, in short, very much resolved on being seriously accepted as soon as possible....She tried to stop him, but vainly; he would go on, and say it all. Angry as she was, the thought of the moment made her resolve to restrain herself when she did speak. She felt that half this folly must be drunkenness, and therefore could hope that it might belong only to the passing hour.

MR. ELTON PROPOSES TO EMMA WOODHOUSE
Emma

UNFOUNDED CONCEIT

John Thorpe…was a stout young man of middling height, who, with a plain face and ungraceful form, seemed fearful of being too handsome unless he wore the dress of a groom, and too much like a gentleman unless he were easy where he ought to be civil, and impudent where he might be allowed to be easy.

Little as Catherine was in the habit of judging for herself, and unfixed as were her general notions of what men ought to be, she could not entirely repress a doubt, while she bore with the effusions of his endless conceit, of his being altogether completely agreeable. It was a bold surmise, for he was Isabella's brother; and she had been assured by [her brother] James that his manners would recommend him to all her sex; but in spite of this, the extreme weariness of his company, which crept over her before they had been out an hour, and which continued unceasingly to increase till they stopped in Pultney Street again, induced her, in some small degree, to resist such high authority, and to distrust his powers of giving universal pleasure.

ON CATHERINE MORLAND'S ADMIRER
JOHN THORPE
Northanger Abbey

*A*T CROSS PURPOSES

"In vain have I struggled. It will not do. My feelings will not be repressed. You must allow me to tell you how ardently I admire and love you."

Elizabeth's astonishment was beyond expression. She stared, coloured, doubted, and was silent. This he considered sufficient encouragement, and the avowal of all that he felt and had long felt for her immediately followed. He spoke well, but there were feelings besides those of the heart to be detailed, and he was not more eloquent on the subject of tenderness than of pride. His sense of her inferiority—of its being a degradation—of the family obstacles which judgment had always opposed to inclination were dwelt on with a warmth which seemed due to the consequence he was wounding, but was very unlikely to recommend his suit.

"In such cases as this [she replied], it is, I believe, the established mode to express a sense of obligation for the sentiments avowed, however unequally they may be returned....But I cannot—I have never desired your good opinion, and you have certainly bestowed it most unwillingly. I am sorry to have occasioned pain to anyone. It has been most unconsciously done, however, and I hope will be of short duration. The feelings which, you tell me, have long prevented the acknowledgment of your regard can have little difficulty in overcoming it after this explanation."

Suitors

Mr. Darcy, who was leaning against the mantelpiece with his eyes fixed on her face, seemed to catch her words with no less resentment than surprise. His complexion became pale with anger, and the disturbance of his mind was visible in every feature. He was struggling for the appearance of composure, and would not open his lips till he believed himself to have attained it. The pause was to Elizabeth's feelings dreadful. At length, in a voice of forced calmness, he said, "And this is all the reply which I am to have the honour of expecting! I might, perhaps, wish to be informed why, with so little *endeavour* at civility, I am thus rejected."

"I might as well inquire," replied she, "why with so evident a design of offending and insulting me you chose to tell me that you liked me against your will, against your reason, and even against your character? Was not this some excuse for incivility, if I *was* uncivil?"

MR. DARCY'S FIRST PROPOSAL TO
ELIZABETH BENNET
Pride and Prejudice

Fortunately for these patient heroines, "Mr. Right" eventually does appear—or reappear. Even a rejected suitor may be given a second chance.

A YOUTHFUL ATTACHMENT RENEWED

I can listen no longer in silence. I must speak to you by such means as are within my reach. You pierce my soul. I am half agony, half hope. Tell me not that I am too late, that such precious feelings are gone forever. I offer myself to you again with a heart even more your own than when you almost broke it, eight years and a half ago. Dare not say that man forgets sooner than woman, that his love has an earlier death. I have loved none but you.…For you alone, I think and plan. Have you not seen this? Can you fail to have understood my wishes?…Too good, too excellent creature! You do us justice, indeed. You do believe there is true attachment and constancy among men. Believe it to be most fervent, most undeviating in

'F. W.'

CAPTAIN WENTWORTH'S LETTER TO ANNE ELLIOT
Persuasion

A BROKEN ENGAGEMENT BRINGS FREEDOM

Unaccountable, however, as the circumstances of his release might appear to the whole family, it was certain that Edward was free; and to what purpose that freedom would be employed was easily predetermined by all;—for after experiencing the blessings of *one* imprudent engagement, contracted without his mother's consent, as he had already done for more than four years, nothing less could be expected of him in the failure of *that*, than the immediate contraction of another.

His errand to Barton, in fact, was a simple one. It was only to ask Elinor to marry him;—and considering that he was not altogether inexperienced in such a question, it might be strange that he should feel so uncomfortable in the present case as he really did, so much in need of encouragement and fresh air.

How soon he had walked himself into the proper resolution, however, how soon an opportunity of exercising it occurred, in what manner he expressed himself, and how he was received, need not be particularly told. This need only be said;—that when they all sat down to table at four o'clock, about three hours after his arrival, he had secured his lady, engaged her mother's consent, and was not only in the rapturous profession of the lover, but in the reality of reason and truth, one of the happiest of men.

EDWARD PROPOSES TO ELINOR
Sense and Sensibility

SINCERITY WINS OUT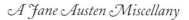

"I cannot make speeches, Emma," he soon resumed, and in a tone of such sincere, decided, intelligible tenderness as was tolerably convincing. "If I loved you less, I might be able to talk about it more. But you know what I am. You hear nothing but truth from me. I have blamed you, and lectured you, and you have borne it as no other woman in England would have borne it. Bear with the truths I would tell you now, dearest Emma, as well as you have borne with them. The manner, perhaps, may have as little to recommend them. God knows, I have been a very indifferent lover. But you understand me. Yes, you see, you understand my feelings—and will return them if you can. At present, I ask only to hear—once more to hear your voice."

MR. KNIGHTLEY DECLARES HIMSELF AT LAST
Emma

A BETTER UNDERSTANDING

"You are too generous to trifle with me. If your feelings are what they were last April, tell me so at once. *My* affections and wishes are unchanged, but one word from you will silence me on this subject forever."

Elizabeth, feeling all the more than common awkwardness and anxiety of his situation, now forced herself to speak; and immediately, though not very fluently, gave him to understand that her sentiments had undergone so material a change, since the period to which he alluded, as to make her receive with gratitude and pleasure his present assurances. The happiness which this reply produced was such as he had probably never felt before; and he expressed himself on the occasion as sensibly and warmly as a man violently in love can be supposed to do. Had Elizabeth been able to encounter his eye, she might have seen how well the expression of heart-felt delight, diffused over his face, became him; but though she could not look, she could listen, and he told her of feelings, which, in proving of what importance she was to him, made his affection every moment more valuable.

MR. DARCY'S SECOND PROPOSAL TO
ELIZABETH BENNET
Pride and Prejudice

A Jane Austen Miscellany

Perceptions change, becoming clearer or more ambivalent as relationships deepen and characters move beyond the constraints of mannered society.

$\mathcal{D}$AWNING ADMIRATION

Mr. Darcy had at first scarcely allowed [Elizabeth] to be pretty; he had looked at her without admiration at the ball; and when they next met, he looked at her only to criticize. But no sooner had he made it clear to himself and his friends that she had hardly a good feature in her face, than he began to find it was rendered uncommonly intelligent by the beautiful expression of her dark eyes. To this discovery succeeded some others equally mortifying. Though he had detected with a critical eye more than one failure of perfect symmetry in her form, he was forced to acknowledge her figure to be light and pleasing; and in spite of his assertion that her manners were not those of the fashionable world, he was caught by their easy playfulness.

> ON DARCY'S GROWING INTEREST IN
> ELIZABETH BENNETT
> *Pride and Prejudice*

Suitors

$\mathcal{A}$ TIMELESS OBSERVATION

Who can be in doubt of what followed? When any two young people take it in to their heads to marry, they are pretty sure by perseverance to carry their point, be they ever so poor, or ever so imprudent, or ever so little likely to be necessary to each other's comfort. This may be bad morality to conclude with, but I believe it to be truth.

ON YOUTHFUL MARRIAGES
Persuasion

$\mathcal{M}$ IXED FEELINGS

Anne, as she sat near the window, descried, most decidedly and distinctly, Captain Wentworth walking down the street.

She now felt a great inclination to go to the outer door; she wanted to see if it rained. Why was she to suspect herself of another motive? Captain Wentworth must be out of sight. She left her seat, she would go; one half of her should not be always so much wiser than the other half, or always suspecting the other of being worse than it was. She would see if it rained.

ON ANNE ELLIOT'S RENEWED HOPES OF
CAPTAIN WENTWORTH'S AFFECTION
Persuasion

Radical Changes

Marianne Dashwood was born to an extraordinary fate. She was born to discover the falsehood of her own opinions, and to counteract, by her conduct, her most favourite maxims. She was born to overcome an affection formed so late in life as at seventeen, and with no sentiment superior to strong esteem and lively friendship, voluntarily to give her hand to another!—and *that* other, a man who had suffered no less than herself under the event of a former attachment, whom two years before, she had considered too old to be married,—and who still sought the constitutional safeguard of a flannel waistcoat!

ON MARIANNE DASHWOOD AND
COLONEL BRANDON
Sense and Sensibility

About-face

"Good gracious! Mr. Darcy!—Well, any friend of Mr. Bingley's will always be welcome here to be sure; but else I must say that I hate the very sight of him."

"Good gracious! Lord bless me! only think! dear me! Mr. Darcy! Who would have thought it! And is it really true? Oh my sweetest Lizzy! how rich and how great you will be! What pin-money, what jewels, what carriages you will have! Jane's is nothing—nothing at all. I am so pleased—so happy. Such a charming man! — so handsome! so tall!— Oh, my dear Lizzy! pray apologize for my having disliked him so much before. I hope he will overlook it. Dear, dear Lizzy. A house in town! Everything that is charming!"

> MRS. BENNET ON MR. DARCY BEFORE AND
> AFTER THE ENGAGEMENT
> *Pride and Prejudice*

*U*NSTABLE AFFECTIONS

If Emma had still, at intervals, an anxious feeling for Harriet, a momentary doubt of its being possible for her to be really cured of her attachment to Mr. Knightley, and really able to accept another man from unbiased inclination, it was not long that she had to suffer from the recurrence of any such uncertainty. A very few days brought the party from London; and she had no sooner an opportunity of being one hour alone with Harriet, than she became perfectly satisfied, unaccountable as it was, that Robert Martin had thoroughly supplanted Mr. Knightley; and was now forming all her views of happiness.

> ON HARRIET SMITH'S ENGAGEMENT TO
> ROBERT MARTIN
> *Emma*

· III ·

Families

A Jane Austen Miscellany

*Family members in Austen's world often focus on their own con-
cerns, to the neglect of those around them. One's place in such a
family can be uncertain, as characters who think and feel deeply
are discounted by those who are shallow and self-seeking.*

CAPTIVATED BY APPEARANCES

Vanity was the beginning and end of Sir Walter Elliot's
character: vanity of person and of situation.

His good looks and his rank had one fair claim on his
attachment, since to them he must have owed a wife of very
superior character to anything deserved by his own. Lady
Elliot had been an excellent woman, sensible and amiable,
whose judgment and conduct, if they might be pardoned
the youthful infatuation which made her Lady Elliot, had
never required indulgence afterwards....Three girls, the
two eldest sixteen and fourteen, was an awful legacy for a
mother to bequeath [upon her untimely death], an awful
charge rather, to confide to the authority of a conceited,
silly father.

UPON LADY ELLIOT'S MISJUDGMENT IN MARRIAGE
Persuasion

$\mathcal{A}$ DOMINEERING MOTHER

After a proper resistance on the part of Mrs. Ferrars, just so violent and so steady as to preserve her from that reproach which she always seemed fearful of incurring, the reproach of being too amiable, Edward was admitted to her presence, and pronounced to be again her son.

Her family had of late been exceedingly fluctuating. For many years of her life she had had two sons; but the crime and annihilation of Edward a few weeks ago, had robbed her of one; the similar annihilation of Robert had left her for a fortnight without any; and now, by the resuscitation of Edward, she had one again.

In spite of his being allowed once more to live, however, he did not feel the continuance of his existence secure, till he had revealed his present engagement; for the publication of that circumstance, he feared, might give a sudden turn to his constitution, and carry him off as rapidly as before.

ON EDWARD FERRARS'S ENGAGEMENT TO
ELINOR DASHWOOD
Sense and Sensibility

A SHY COUSIN JOINS THE FAMILY

Fanny Price was at this time just ten years old, and though there might not be much in her first appearance to captivate, there was, at least, nothing to disgust her relations....Sir Thomas and Lady Bertram received her very kindly; and Sir Thomas, seeing how much she needed encouragement, tried all that was conciliating; but he had to work against a most untoward gravity of deportment; and Lady Bertram, without taking half so much trouble, or speaking one word where he spoke ten, by the mere aid of a good-humoured smile, became immediately the less awful character of the two.

They were a remarkably fine family, the sons very well-looking, the daughters decidedly handsome, and all of them well-grown and forward of their age, which produced as striking a difference between the cousins in person, as education had given to their address; and no one would have supposed the girls so nearly of an age as they really were. There was in fact but two years between the youngest and Fanny.

FANNY PRICE MEETS HER RELATIVES,
THE BERTRAMS
Mansfield Park

A DEARTH OF AFFECTION

Elizabeth had succeeded at sixteen to all that was possible of her mother's rights and consequence; and being very handsome, and very like himself [her father], her influence had always been great, and they had gone on together most happily. His two other children were of very inferior value. Mary had acquired a little artificial importance by becoming Mrs. Charles Musgrove; but Anne, with an elegance of mind and sweetness of character, which must have placed her high with any people of real understanding, was nobody with either father or sister; her word had no weight, her convenience was always to give way—she was only Anne.

ON SIR WALTER ELLIOT'S VALUATION OF
HIS YOUNGER DAUGHTERS
Persuasion

*A*CQUAINTANCES FORMED AT BATH

Mrs. Thorpe was a widow, and not a very rich one; she was a good-humoured, well-meaning woman, and a very indulgent mother. Her eldest daughter had great personal beauty, and the younger ones, by pretending to be as handsome as their sister, imitating her air, and dressing in the same style, did very well.

> ON ISABELLA THORPE AND
> HER YOUNGER SISTERS
> *Northanger Abbey*

*A*N UNSUITABLE MARRIAGE

Mr. Bennet was so odd a mixture of quick parts, sarcastic humour, reserve, and caprice, that the experience of three-and-twenty years had been insufficient to make his wife understand his character. *Her* mind was less difficult to develop. She was a woman of mean understanding, little information, and uncertain temper. When she was discontented, she fancied herself nervous. The business of her life was to get her daughters married; its solace was visiting and news.

> ON THE RELATIONSHIP BETWEEN
> MR. AND MRS. BENNET
> *Pride and Prejudice*

*G*RIEF AND RESOLUTION

Elinor saw, with concern, the excess of her sister's sensibility; but by Mrs. Dashwood it was valued and cherished. They encouraged each other now in the violence of their affliction. The agony of grief which overpowered them at first, was voluntarily renewed, was sought for, was created again and again. They gave themselves up wholly to their sorrow, seeking increase of wretchedness in every reflection that could afford it, and resolved against ever admitting consolation in future. Elinor, too, was deeply afflicted; but still she could struggle, she could exert herself. She could consult with her brother, could receive her sister-in-law on her arrival, and treat her with every proper attention; and could strive to rouse her mother to similar exertion, and encourage her to similar forbearance.

ON MR. DASHWOOD'S DEATH
Sense and Sensibility

In Austen's world, the vicissitudes of family fortunes and the behaviour of one's relatives inevitably reflect—however unjustly—on the status of the individual. Austen's heroines often find the shortcomings of their relatives to be a cause of embarrassment or unease.

$\mathcal{D}$ISTRESSING REFLECTIONS

To Elizabeth it appeared that had her family made an agreement to expose themselves as much as they could during the evening, it would have been impossible for them to play their parts with more spirit or finer success; and happy did she think it for Bingley and her sister that some of the exhibition had escaped his notice, and that his feelings were not of a sort to be much distressed by the folly which he must have witnessed. That his two sisters and Mr. Darcy, however, should have such an opportunity of ridiculing her relations was bad enough, and she could not determine whether the silent contempt of the gentleman, or the insolent smiles of the ladies, were more intolerable.

AT THE NETHERFIELD BALL
Pride and Prejudice

$\mathcal{A}$ LACK OF SOLIDARITY

Anne, satisfied at a very early period of Lady Russell's meaning to love Captain Wentworth as she ought, had no other alloy to the happiness of her prospects than what arose from the consciousness of having no relations to bestow on him which a man of sense could value. There she felt her own inferiority keenly. The disproportion in their fortune was nothing; it did not give her a moment's regret; but to have no family to receive and estimate him properly, nothing of respectability, of harmony, of good-will, to offer in return for all the worth and all the proper welcome which met her in his brothers and sisters, was a source of as lively pain as her mind could well be sensible of under circumstances of otherwise strong felicity.

> ON ANNE ELLIOT'S FIRST ENGAGEMENT TO
> CAPTAIN WENTWORTH
> *Persuasion*

$\mathcal{J}$ USTIFIABLE CRITICISM

In her own behaviour, there was a constant source of vexation and regret; and in the unhappy defects of her family a subject of yet heavier chagrin. They were hopeless of remedy. Her father, contented with laughing at them, would never exert himself to restrain the wild giddiness of his youngest daughters; and their mother, with manners so far from right herself, was entirely insensible of the evil. Elizabeth had frequently united with Jane in an endeavour to check the imprudence of Catherine and Lydia; but while they were supported by their mother's indulgence, what chance could there be of improvement?

When she came to that part of the letter in which her family were mentioned, in terms of such mortifying, yet merited reproach, her sense of shame was severe. The justice of the charge struck her too forcibly for denial, and the circumstances to which he particularly alluded, as having passed at the Netherfield ball, and as confirming all his first disapprobation, could not have made a stronger impression on his mind than on hers.

The compliment to herself and her sister was not unfelt. It soothed, but it could not console her for the contempt which had been thus self-attracted by the rest of her family; and as she considered that Jane's disappointment had in fact been the work of her nearest relations, and reflected how materially the credit of both must be hurt by such impropriety of conduct, she felt depressed beyond anything she had ever known before.

ELIZABETH BENNET READS MR. DARCY'S LETTER
Pride and Prejudice

Austen's more fortunate heroines are blessed with family members whose solid worth and respectability are a source of pride.

GOOD SENSE AND GOOD HUMOUR

No one who had ever seen Catherine Morland in her infancy would have supposed her born to be an heroine. Her situation in life, the character of her father and mother, her own person and disposition, were equally against her. Her father was a clergyman, without being neglected or poor, and a very respectable man, though his name was Richard, and he had never been handsome. He had a considerable independence, besides two good livings, and he was not in the least addicted to locking up his daughters. Her mother was a woman of useful plain sense, with a good temper, and, what is more remarkable, with good constitution. She had three sons before Catherine was born; and, instead of dying in bringing the latter into the world, as anybody might expect, she still lived on—lived to have six children more—to see them growing up around her, and to enjoy excellent health herself.

ON CATHERINE MORLAND'S FAMILY
Northanger Abbey

ON THE CREDIT SIDE

Mr. Gardiner was a sensible, gentlemanlike man, greatly superior to his sister as well by nature as [by] education. The Netherfield ladies would have had difficulty in believing that a man who lived by trade, and within view of his own warehouses, could have been so well bred and agreeable. Mrs. Gardiner, who was several years younger than Mrs. Bennet and [her sister] Mrs. Phillips, was an amiable, intelligent, elegant woman, and a great favourite with all her Longbourn nieces. Between the two eldest and herself there subsisted a very particular regard.

ON MRS. BENNET'S BROTHER AND HIS WIFE
Pride and Prejudice

Friends

Austen held friendship in high esteem, and her novels give many examples of both true friendship and its counterfeits among characters of many types.

A FOLLOWER AND A LEADER

Between him and Darcy there was a very steady friendship, in spite of a great opposition of character. Bingley was endeared to Darcy by the easiness, openness, and ductility of his temper, though no disposition could offer a greater contrast to his own, and though with his own he never seemed dissatisfied. On the strength of Darcy's regard Bingley had the firmest reliance, and of his judgment the highest opinion. In understanding, Darcy was the superior. Bingley was by no means deficient, but Darcy was clever. He was at the same time haughty, reserved, and fastidious, and his manners, though well bred, were not inviting. In that respect his friend had greatly the advantage. Bingley was sure of being liked wherever he appeared, Darcy was continually giving offence.

ON CHARLES BINGLEY AND FITZWILLIAM DARCY
Pride and Prejudice

*A*FFINITY OF TASTE AND CHARACTER

In Colonel Brandon alone, of all her new acquaintance, did Elinor find a person who could in any degree claim the respect of abilities, excite the interest of friendship, or give pleasure as a companion. Willoughby was out of the question. Her admiration and regard, even her sisterly regard, was all his own; but he was a lover; his attentions were wholly Marianne's, and a far less agreeable man might have been more generally pleasing. Colonel Brandon, unfortunately for himself, had no such encouragement to think only of Marianne, and in conversing with Elinor he found the greatest consolation for the total indifference of her sister.

ON ELINOR DASHWOOD AND COLONEL BRANDON
Sense and Sensibility

A BALANCED PERSPECTIVE

Mr. Knightley, a sensible man about seven or eight-and-thirty, was not only a very old and intimate friend of the family, but particularly connected with it, as the elder brother of Isabella's husband. He lived about a mile from Highbury, was a frequent visitor, and was always welcome.

Mr. Knightley, in fact, was one of the few people who could see faults in Emma Woodhouse, and the only one who ever told her of them; and though this was not particularly agreeable to Emma herself, she knew it would be so much less so to her father, that she would not have him really suspect such a circumstance as her not being thought perfect by everyone.

> ON EMMA WOODHOUSE AND GEORGE KNIGHTLEY
> *Emma*

A FRIEND IN NEED

The comfort of such a friend at that moment as Colonel Brandon—of such a companion for her mother,—how gratefully was it felt!—a companion whose judgment would guide, whose attendance must relieve, and whose friendship might soothe her!—as far as the shock of such a summons *could* be lessened to her, his presence, his manners, his assistance, would lessen it.

> ELINOR DASHWOOD'S THOUGHTS UPON
> MARIANNE'S ILLNESS
> *Sense and Sensibility*

Friends

*T*HROWN TOGETHER BY CIRCUMSTANCE

This specimen of the Miss Steeles was enough. The vulgar freedom and folly of the eldest left her with no recommendation, and as Elinor was not blinded by the beauty, or the shrewd look of the youngest, to her want of real elegance and artlessness, she left the house without any wish of knowing them better.

Not so, the Miss Steeles.—They came from Exeter, well provided with admiration for the use of Sir John Middleton, his family, and all his relations, and no niggardly proportion was now dealt out to his fair cousins, whom they declared to be the most beautiful, elegant, accomplished and agreeable girls they had ever beheld, and with whom they were particularly anxious to be better acquainted.—And to be better acquainted therefore, Elinor soon found was their inevitable lot....

ELINOR DASHWOOD ON THE MISS STEELES
Sense and Sensibility

A Jane Austen Miscellany

Noblesse Oblige

Harriet Smith was the natural daughter of somebody. Somebody had placed her, several years back, at Mrs. Goddard's school, and somebody had lately raised her from the condition of scholar to that of parlour border. This was all that was generally known of her history. She had no visible friends, but what had been acquired at Highbury….

[Emma] was not struck by anything remarkably clever in Miss Smith's conversation, but she found her altogether very engaging….*She* would notice her; she would improve her; she would detach her from her bad acquaintances, and introduce her into good society; she would form her opinions and manners. It would be an interesting, and certainly a very kind undertaking; highly becoming her own situation in life, her leisure, and powers.

Harriet certainly was not clever, but she had a sweet, docile, grateful disposition, was totally free from conceit, and only desiring to be guided by anyone she looked up to….Altogether she was quite convinced of Harriet Smith's being exactly the young friend she wanted—exactly the something which her home required.

EMMA WOODHOUSE TAKES UP HARRIET SMITH
Emma

Friends

*I*NSTANT INTIMACY—AND ITS EROSION

The whole being explained, many obliging things were said by the Miss Thorpes of their wish of being better acquainted with her; of being considered as already friends, through the friendship of their brothers, etc., which Catherine heard with pleasure, and answered with all the pretty expressions she could command; and, as the first proof of amity, she was soon invited to accept the arm of the eldest Miss Thorpe, and take a turn with her about the Room. Catherine was delighted with this extension of her Bath acquaintance, and almost forgot Mr. Tilney while she talked to Miss Thorpe. Friendship is certainly the finest balm for the pangs of disappointed love.

The progress of the friendship between Catherine and Isabella was quick as its beginning had been warm; and they passed so rapidly through every gradation of increasing tenderness, that there was shortly no fresh proof of it to be given to their friends or themselves. They called each other by their Christian names, were always arm-in-arm when they walked, pinned up each other's train for the dance, and were not to be divided in the set; and, if a rainy morning deprived them of other enjoyments, they were still resolute in meeting in defiance of wet and dirt, and shut themselves up to read novels together.

Catherine was distressed, but not subdued. "Do not urge me Isabella. I am engaged to Miss Tilney. I cannot go." This availed nothing. The same arguments assailed her again; she must go, she should go, and they would not hear of a refusal.

"It would be so easy to tell Miss Tilney that you had just been reminded of a prior engagement, and must beg to put off the walk till Tuesday."

"No, it would not be easy. I could not do it. There has been no prior engagement." But Isabella became only more and more urgent; calling on her in the most affectionate manner; addressing her by the most endearing names. She was sure her dearest, sweetest Catherine would not seriously refuse such a trifling request to a friend who loved her so dearly. She knew her beloved Catherine to have so feeling a heart, so sweet a temper, to be easily persuaded by those she loved…. Isabella then tried another method. She reproached her with having more affection for Miss Tilney, though she had known her so little a while, than for her best and oldest friends; with being grown cold and indifferent, in short, towards herself.

CATHERINE MORLAND AND ISABELLA THORPE
Northanger Abbey

ᏚNOBBERY RAMPANT

A widow Mrs. Smith, lodging in Westgate Buildings! A poor widow, barely able to live, between thirty and forty; a mere Mrs. Smith, an every-day Mrs. Smith, of all people and all names in the world, to be the chosen friend of Miss Anne Elliot, and to be preferred by her to her own family connections among the nobility of England and Ireland! Mrs. Smith! Such a name!

Mrs. Clay, who had been present while all this passed, now thought it advisable to leave the room, and Anne could have said much, and did long to say a little in defence of her friend's not very dissimilar claims to theirs, but her sense of personal respect to her father prevented her. She made no reply. She left it to himself to recollect, that Mrs. Smith was not the only widow in Bath between thirty and forty, with little to live, and no surname of dignity.

SIR WALTER ELLIOT'S OBJECTION TO
HIS DAUGHTER'S NEW FRIEND
Persuasion

*I*NFLUENCE VS. AFFECTION

"You expect me to account for opinions which you choose to call mine, but which I have never acknowledged. Allowing the case, however, to stand according to your representation, you must remember, Miss Bennet, that the friend who is supposed to desire his return to the house, and the delay of his plan, has merely desired it, asked it without offering one argument in favour of its propriety."

"To yield readily—easily—to the *persuasion* of a friend is no merit with you."

"To yield without conviction is no compliment to the understanding of either."

"You appear to me, Mr. Darcy, to allow nothing for the influence of friendship and affection. A regard for the requester would often make one readily yield to a request, without waiting for arguments to reason one into it."

> MR. DARCY AND ELIZABETH BENNET
> ON FRIENDSHIP
> *Pride and Prejudice*

Friends

A FRIENDSHIP DISAPPROVED

But Harriet Smith—I have not half done about Harriet Smith. I think her the very worst sort of companion that Emma could possibly have. She knows nothing herself, and looks upon Emma as knowing everything. She is a flatterer in all her ways; and so much the worse, because undesigned. Her ignorance is hourly flattery. How can Emma imagine she has anything to learn herself, while Harriet is presenting such a delightful inferiority? And as for Harriet, I will venture to say that *she* will not gain by the acquaintance. Hartfield will only put her out of conceit with all the other places she belongs to. She will grow just refined enough to be uncomfortable with those among whom birth and circumstances have placed her home.

> MR. KNIGHTLEY ON EMMA WOODHOUSE
> AND HARRIET SMITH
> *Emma*

*D*ISARMING NAIVETÉ

Catherine's understanding began to awake; an idea of the truth suddenly darted into her mind; and with the natural blush of so new an emotion, she cried out, "Good heaven! my dear Isabella, what do you mean? Can you—can you really be in love with James?"

This bold surmise, however, she soon learnt comprehended but half the fact. The anxious affection which she was accused of having continually watched in Isabella's every look and action, had, in the course of their yesterday's party, received the delightful confession of an equal love. Her heart and faith were alike engaged to James. Never had Catherine listened to anything so full of interest, wonder, and joy. Her brother and her friend engaged! New to such circumstances, the importance of it appeared unspeakably great, and she contemplated it as one of those grand events of which the ordinary course of life can hardly afford a return.

ON ISABELLA THORP'S ENGAGEMENT TO
CATHERINE MORLAND'S BROTHER JAMES
Northanger Abbey